ANNE ROCKWELL

THE ROBBER BABY

STORIES FROM THE GREEK MYTHS

GREENWILLOW BOOKS, NEW YORK

**IN MEMORY OF SAMUEL HOWARD
AND FOR MY GRANDCHILDREN,
NICHOLAS HARLOW, JULIANNA JOY, AND NIGEL JOHN**

Thanks to Father Robert J. Miner
for his help with the pronunciation guide

Serigraphs hand painted with watercolors were used
for the full-color art. The text type is Cochin.

Printed in Singapore by Tien Wah Press
First Edition 10 9 8 7 6 5 4 3 2 1

Library of Congress Cataloging-in-Publication Data

Rockwell, Anne F.
The robber baby: stories from the Greek myths /
by Anne Rockwell.
p. cm.
Summary: Retells fifteen tales from Greek mythology, including the stories of Hermes, Demeter and Kore, Daedalus, Atalanta, and Pandora.
ISBN 0-688-09740-5 (trade).
ISBN 0-688-09741-3 (lib. bdg.)
1. Mythology, Greek—Juvenile literature.
[1. Mythology, Greek.] I. Title.
BL782.R63 1994
398.2′0938—dc20
90-39560 CIP AC

CONTENTS

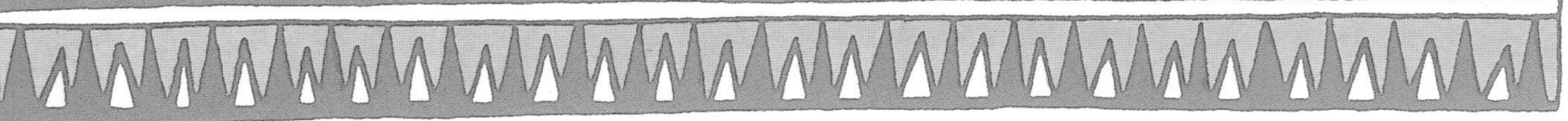

THE GODS

In ancient Greece, the people believed that various gods and goddesses ruled their lives. Twelve of the most important of these gods and goddesses sat on golden thrones on the top of Mount Olympus. These twelve gods and goddesses were sometimes called The Twelve, but more often they were called The Immortal Ones, for, unlike mortal people who lived and died, none of the gods and goddesses ever died. But in many other ways, The Immortal Ones were much like the people who worshiped them. The Twelve who sat on golden thrones on Mount Olympus were named Zeus, Hera, Apollo, Artemis, Athene, Aphrodite, Ares, Hephaestus, Hermes, Demeter, Poseidon, and Dionysus.

Zeus was the ruler of the gods. Only mighty Zeus could throw the thunderbolt and hold the scales of justice. The eagle was his favorite bird. Hera was his wife, but theirs was not a happy marriage. Though Hera was the goddess of marriage, she was never thought of as a loving wife or a kind mother. Instead,

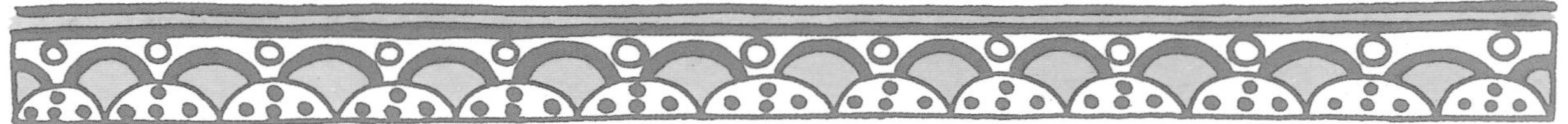

she was vain, arrogant, and jealous. Hera's favorite bird was the peacock, for it strutted proudly about, just as she did.

Zeus had twin children, a boy and a girl, but Hera was not their mother. Each of them had a golden throne. Apollo, the brother, was the god of music and mathematics, poetry, medicine, and healing. He was also the god of light, and he ruled over the sun. Apollo's twin sister, Artemis, was the goddess of the hunt and the wild beasts of the forest. She was the goddess who watched over women when they gave birth, and she protected little children. She also ruled the moon.

Athene, the goddess of wisdom, was another daughter of Zeus. In fact, Athene had no mother. It was said she had been born, wearing shining armor, from the forehead of Zeus himself. Athene looked warlike, but she was the goddess of peace. And she was the goddess who watched over cities and the mortals who lived in them. Athene loved the little owl, for it was as wise as she was, and she carried an olive branch as a sign that she came to bring peace.

Aphrodite was the goddess of love. All of the goddesses were beautiful, but none was as beautiful as Aphrodite. She was usually accompanied by her son, Eros. Eros was a plump and fun-loving baby with wings that sprouted from his shoulders. Unfortunately, he also had a little golden bow and a quiver full of tiny golden arrows. He used these to cause all kinds of mischief among mortals. For when anyone was shot with an arrow of Eros, he or she would fall in love with the next person seen, however unsuitable that person might be.

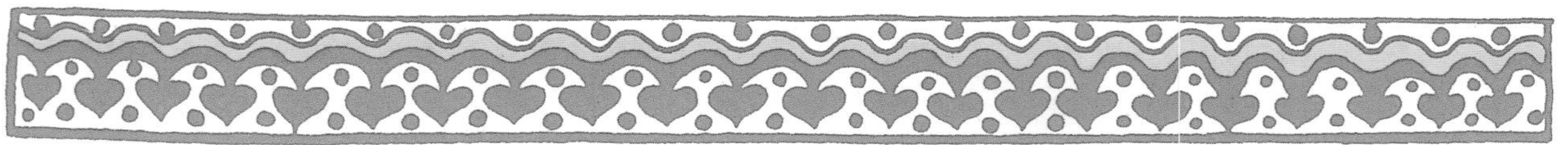

Ares was the god of war. He was the only child of the unhappy marriage of Zeus and Hera. Among the other Olympians, only Aphrodite cared for Ares, for he was a cruel troublemaker who loved the noise and death of the battlefield.

Hephaestus was the god of craft and mechanical invention. He invented every mechanical device in the world, and he made every beautiful object there was, before any mortal artist or craftsman did.

There were times when Zeus had to send messages to people below, and so, like any king, he had a royal messenger. This messenger brought dreams to mortals, and he also came to be with them when they died. His name was Hermes.

Demeter was the great goddess who made things grow for the mortals on earth. She had a young daughter named Kore whom she loved dearly.

Zeus had two brothers. One was Poseidon, the god of the sea. Poseidon had a golden throne on Mount Olympus, although he seldom sat on it, for he preferred his own kingdom beneath the sea. The other was Hades. Hades was a very great god, but he did not have a throne on Mount Olympus. Instead, he had a throne in his own kingdom, the kingdom of the underworld, where the dead were taken by Hermes. Hades had a helmet that made him invisible so he could come among mortals and not be seen. He was a dreaded and hated god.

Hestia was the goddess of the hearth. She tended the fire where the gods and goddesses kept warm and prepared their meals. Her job was so important that she had a golden throne.

She was a quiet goddess who never caused trouble for anyone.

But one day a new god came to Mount Olympus. This new god was the son of Zeus and a mother who had died. Hera had been so jealous of the mother that she hated the new god. But Zeus wanted this son of his to have his own throne on Mount Olympus. So kindhearted Hestia gave him hers. The new god was called Dionysus, and he was the god of wine.

These gods were worshiped not only by the Greeks but also by the Romans in a later time. We know many of them by their Roman names as well. To the Romans, Zeus was Jupiter, Hera was Juno, Athene was Minerva, Hermes was Mercury, Hephaestus was Vulcan, and Ares was Mars. Aphrodite and her son Eros were Venus and Cupid. Demeter was known as Ceres, and Hestia was called Vesta by the Romans. Artemis was called Diana, and Dionysus was called Bacchus. Poseidon was known as Neptune. His brother Hades was called Pluto by the Romans. But to the Romans Pluto was not as much the hated god of the underworld as the god who owned all the riches buried in the earth. And Apollo was always called by his Greek name.

Besides the great gods of Mount Olympus, there were other gods and goddesses who lived on earth in ancient Greece. The greatest of these was Pan, the god of wild goats and of wild and crazy behavior.

Zeus had nine daughters called the Muses. Their mother was Mnemosyne, the goddess of memory. The Muses were the goddesses of poetry and song and history and storytelling, and they were Apollo's helpers. Whenever a mortal wished to tell a

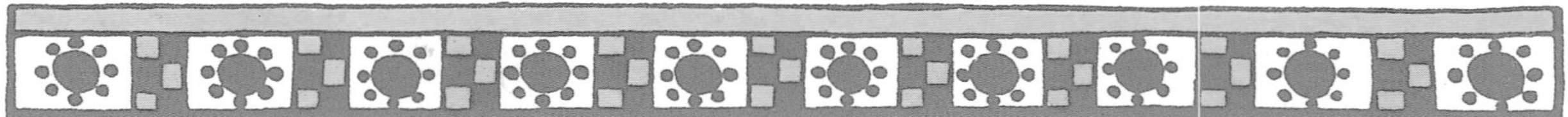

story about one of the gods or goddesses, the storyteller would ask one of the Muses for inspiration.

In addition to the gods and goddesses and the mortals who worshiped them, there were also beings such as nymphs, who were spirits of nature. Often nymphs were the daughters of rivers. They usually lived longer than mortals, but they were still subject to death.

There were other mortals whose deeds were so remarkable that they almost seemed like gods, but they were not. These mortals were especially favored by the gods and were called heroes.

Stories about gods and goddesses, nymphs, ordinary mortals, and great heroes are called myths. The stories in this book are some of the myths of ancient Greece. They are stories that people have told and written down for others to read for many centuries.

Hermes was not only the messenger of the gods but also the god of reading and writing. So it is fitting that this book should begin with a story about him.

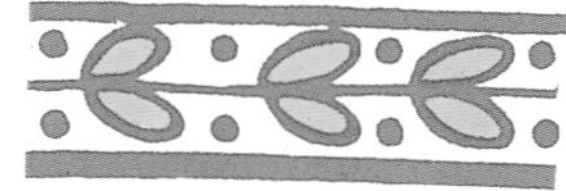

THE ROBBER BABY

Hermes was always full of mischief. On the very day that he was born, while his mother, the nymph Maia, was having a nap, he got up from his cradle. Then he sneaked out of the cave where he lived and stole fifty cows from the god Apollo.

He made shoes from the bark of oak trees for each of the four feet of the fifty cows. Then he put the shoes on their feet backward. That way, anyone trying to find the cows by following their footprints would think the cows had walked in the opposite direction. Then, so no one could recognize his own footsteps, Hermes made sandals for himself out of reeds. These sandals made footprints that looked like nothing ever seen on earth, prints that looked as if the trees had gone walking.

On his way home, the clever baby found a tortoise shell. "I like that," he said to himself as he admired its interesting shape. And so he kept it.

As soon as he got home, Hermes slaughtered two of the cows. He made an offering to the gods and lunch for himself. Then he made the two hides of the cows into leather. He cut seven strips of leather and made himself a lyre by stretching the

strips across the tortoise shell he had found. That lyre was the first musical instrument in the world.

Tricky little Hermes did all this before his mother woke from her nap that afternoon. When his mother did wake up, Hermes pretended to be sound asleep in his basket cradle.

Meanwhile, Apollo had discovered that fifty of his beautiful cows were missing. An old man told him that he had seen a tiny baby leading the cattle away. Apollo knew that the nymph Maia had given birth to a baby, and he immediately suspected that this was the baby who had stolen his cows.

Apollo hurried to the cave where Hermes lived with his mother and demanded his cows back.

"How silly!" said Hermes's mother. "How could my tiny baby steal your cows?"

"Where did he get those leather hides if not from my cows?" shouted Apollo.

At the sound of the god's angry voice, little Hermes woke up. He grinned and rubbed his chubby fingers across the leather strings of the lyre he had made.

Apollo felt his anger disappearing. He was spellbound by the lovely sound of the lyre, and he wanted that lyre more than anything in the world. So he said to Hermes, "I will trade you that lyre for the cows you stole, if you like."

"That is not a bad bargain," said Hermes, with a twinkle in his eye.

Then Hermes decided he wanted to be a god like Apollo. He wanted to sit on a golden throne with Apollo and Zeus and all the other Immortal Ones. He asked Apollo to take him to see mighty Zeus.

On the way to Mount Olympus, Hermes grew very quickly. By the time he and Apollo reached the throne of Zeus, Hermes was a tall young boy. He was not at all in awe of Zeus. He began joking with him, and Zeus was very amused by tricky Hermes.

I would like to have that young fellow here, just for the fun of it, thought Zeus. Besides, he had a strong suspicion that he might be Hermes's father, for he had once loved the nymph Maia, who was his mother. "Very well," he said. "You may come to sit on a throne here on Mount Olympus, if you like. But you must never steal from one of the gods again. And you must never try to deceive me with your lies and tricks!"

Hermes promised Zeus that he would do as he commanded.

"I will give you a job to keep you busy," said Zeus. "I will make you my messenger to the mortals below." And that is exactly what he did.

Zeus gave Hermes a wide-brimmed hat and a cape to protect him from the rain, for he had to travel in all weather to all sorts of places. Then Hephaestus made him golden sandals with wings and added golden wings to his hat. That was so Hermes

could travel quickly from his throne on Mount Olympus to the earth below whenever Zeus commanded him to do so. Last of all, Zeus gave Hermes a golden staff with snakes twirling around it. Hermes always carried the staff to show that he was the messenger of Zeus himself.

Hermes brought all sorts of messages from Zeus to mortals. Some of them were happy messages, and some were sad. But there was one message that Hermes always hated to deliver. When the time came for someone to die, it was his duty to tell the dying person that he had come to accompany that mortal to the kingdom of Hades.

Hermes and Apollo became the closest of friends. Never again did Hermes steal from Apollo or play any tricks on him. In fact, Hermes invented notes for music and then taught them to Apollo.

Hermes was so clever that he was always thinking up ideas that had never been thought of before. He invented the letters of the alphabet and the way to use them for reading and writing. And he invented ways to weigh and measure things.

Hermes always watched over travelers, for he was one himself. He watched over herds of cattle and the herders who took care of them. He watched over merchants and shopkeepers and all who lived by their wits. He was the god of dreams and lies and clever tricks that were sometimes good and sometimes bad.

And, I am sorry to say, he was the one god who was especially fond of thieves and robbers.

THE MOTHER WHO LOST HER DAUGHTER

Demeter was the goddess of green and growing things. She was good and kind and beautiful, and she had a young daughter named Kore. No mother ever loved a child as much as Demeter loved her Kore.

In those days, it was always summertime, and people on earth were never cold or hungry. But they did not know how to plant seeds. Only Demeter could make things grow. Without her, people would have had no fruit and flowers, or wheat and barley with which to make their bread. But Demeter saw to it that the fields were high and golden with wheat and barley and the trees always bore sweet fruit.

One day her daughter, Kore, was picking flowers in a meadow. Kore danced and sang as she picked the flowers.

Suddenly she stopped dancing and said, "Ohhh, how beautiful!" For Kore saw a strange flower she had never seen before. She ran over to pick it, singing and dancing as she added it to her bouquet.

Far down below in the chilly, dank underworld, Hades, the god who ruled the land of the dead, heard Kore's sweet singing and the sound of her dancing feet.

He decided he wanted the young girl to be his queen. She was full of laughter and joy, and Hades often grew gloomy and lonely in his dark and dismal kingdom, with only the dead for company. He made up his mind to steal Kore away from the flower-filled meadow.

All at once there was a terrible cracking sound. The earth where Kore danced opened wide. Hades rose up from the dark underworld, driving a golden chariot pulled by black horses. He grabbed Kore, lifted her into his chariot, and galloped back to the black hole where the earth had ripped open.

"Mother! Mother! Help me!" the poor girl shrieked as loudly as she could. But Kore had danced so far from where her mother was, that Demeter could not hear her calling. Only a little swineherd tending his pigs saw what happened. He began to cry

as loudly as Kore, because all his pigs tumbled into the black opening in the earth. Then the hole closed behind them.

Demeter searched for her daughter. She ran everywhere calling for her, and when she could not find her, she began to sob and wail. No laughing girl's voice called back to her, "I am coming, Mother."

Kore could not answer, for she was far, far away. Day after day she sat, sad and silent, next to Hades on the throne he had given her in the land of the dead. Her tan and rosy cheeks grew pale and cold. She ate nothing, until one day when she tasted a pomegranate and swallowed one of its tiny, blood-red seeds.

Demeter traveled all over the world searching for her lost child. Her beautiful golden hair, which had been the color of ripe wheat, turned dull and gray. In her grief, the goddess forgot to tell the wheat and barley to grow. So all the stalks of wheat and barley withered. She forgot to tell the trees to bear fruit. So the fruit trees shed their green leaves, and their apples and pears and figs shriveled up and died. The first cold winter in the world came. All the people were hungry. Their children cried, for they

had no bread or fruit to eat and they were cold, besides.

Demeter kept on searching for Kore. She asked everyone she met if they had seen her child. But everyone said no until at last the goddess met a boy called Triptolemus. Triptolemus was the older brother of the little swineherd. Demeter asked Triptolemus, as she asked everyone she met, "Have you seen my lovely child who is lost? Have you seen dear Kore with her golden braids and dancing feet?"

And Triptolemus answered, "I have not seen her, but I know where she is."

Then he told the goddess what his brother had seen that dreadful day.

When Demeter heard what Triptolemus told her, she grew very angry. Since Hades was the brother of Zeus, she went straight up to Mount Olympus and said to mighty Zeus, "Your wicked brother has stolen my child! Make him give her back to me!"

And Demeter, who had always been so kind and gentle, screamed at Zeus so that even he was afraid. Besides, he was sad to see the fruits and grains and grasses of the earth all withered and gone. It was no fun for him to watch the mortals below when they just sat and shivered with cold and hunger.

So Zeus sent Hermes down to the underworld kingdom.

Hermes told Hades that Zeus commanded him to return Kore to her mother. Hades could not refuse to obey the orders of his brother, for Zeus was even more powerful than he. But Hades knew that the girl had eaten the pomegranate seed. The blood-red pomegranate was the fruit of the dead. Anyone who tasted it had to return, sooner or later, to Hades's underworld kingdom.

"I will let her go, since Zeus commands me," said Hades to the messenger god. "But because of the pomegranate seed she ate, she must return to me for part of the year to sit beside me as my wife and queen. Then her name will be Persephone. For that is the name I have chosen for her. Kore is a name for a child, not a queen!"

So Kore, who was now called Persephone, returned to her mother. Demeter was glad and happy again. Once more she told the wheat and barley to grow. She made red poppies appear among the golden wheat and made the trees bear apples and pears and figs. She made the earth put forth all the good things that people needed. It was the first springtime in the world. And everyone was happy again.

But after eight months, Persephone had to say good-bye to her mother and return to her throne beside her husband, King Hades. She had to remain in the cold, damp, dark underworld for four long months. While she was there, she seemed as cold and lifeless as the dead around her, and her husband did not understand why she would not dance and sing for him.

Throughout those four months of every year, Demeter mourns for her child. The wheat and barley wither and die. The red poppy petals fall away, and the trees bear no more fruit. Winter comes. Demeter's tears fall as cold rain and sleet until at last the happy day arrives when her daughter returns to her and springtime begins.

Demeter rewarded Triptolemus well for his help. She gave him a chariot pulled by dragons, a bag of seeds, and a wooden plow. Then she whispered to him the secrets of how to make things grow and how to harvest them and save them so that people would have food to eat through the long winter months.

Triptolemus traveled all over the world in his dragon chariot. He taught the people who would listen to him how to plant and how to harvest and preserve what they had grown. All over the world, people planted the seeds Triptolemus gave them—the gifts of Demeter. The people had bread for the long winter.

When springtime comes, people on earth rejoice with Demeter. Persephone returns to her mother and sings and dances through the fields. Demeter is filled with joy, and all the green things sprout and grow again.

THE HERO AND HIS HORSE

Bellerophon was a mortal, but he was the son of Poseidon, god of the sea. He was very handsome and very brave, and a certain king's wife fell in love with him, even though he did nothing to encourage her.

Bellerophon ignored the queen when she tried to show him how much she loved him. This humiliated her, and to get back at him she made up a lie. She told her husband that the young man had declared his love for her. The king became so jealous he made up his mind to destroy Bellerophon. But he wanted to do it in a way that would hide his crime.

At that time, there lived a terrible monster called the Chimaera. It had the head of a lion, the body of a goat, and the tail of a serpent. No one could kill the Chimaera, for it had a breath of fire that scorched to death anyone who came near it.

The jealous king ordered Bellerophon to kill the Chimaera for him. Bellerophon knew that this was impossible. He also guessed the reason why he had suddenly become the king's enemy. Bellerophon knew that the goddess Athene hated injustice, and so he made an offering to her and asked for her help.

Athene listened to Bellerophon's plea and decided to help

him. The goddess in her bright armor appeared to him in a meadow not far from where the fire-breathing Chimaera lived. She handed Bellerophon a magic bridle made by Hephaestus and said, "A horse named Pegasus grazes in this meadow. Put this bridle on him and ride him and he will help you."

Bellerophon asked, "How will I know him when I see him?"

Athene replied, "It will be impossible not to recognize Pegasus. He is a miraculous horse, as white as the moon. He also has wings and can fly."

No sooner had the goddess disappeared when Bellerophon heard a whinnying sound. A winged horse that was as white as the moon galloped up to him. The horse bowed his head before Bellerophon and allowed himself to be bridled.

No sooner had Bellerophon jumped on the horse's back than Pegasus flew up into the sky. The horse flew over the spot where the dreadful Chimaera was coughing out its fiery breath, but the horse flew high enough so that Bellerophon was safe. The goddess Athene had given him the wisdom to know what to do next. He took his spear and tied a lump of lead to its end. Riding the winged horse, Bellerophon aimed his spear at the Chimaera.

The spear with the lump of lead landed right inside the monster's mouth. As soon as its hot breath touched the lead, the metal melted, poured down the monster's throat, and burned its insides. Soon the terrible Chimaera was dead.

This deed made Bellerophon a great and famous hero. Astride the wonderful winged horse that wore Athene's magic golden bridle, he performed deeds of remarkable bravery. And

his fame spread everywhere. Many mortals began to worship this hero as though he were a god, and Bellerophon began to forget that his heroism was not his doing alone. He forgot about the help that Athene had given him. He decided to ride Pegasus to Mount Olympus and ask for a home among the immortal gods and goddesses.

When Zeus saw Bellerophon and Pegasus flying toward his throne, the great god became very angry at Bellerophon. He sent a big green fly to sting Pegasus. As soon as the fly bit the white horse, Pegasus whinnied with pain and reared. Bellerophon fell from the horse's back, down through the sky.

He landed in a desert, far from any other mortals. Bellerophon understood that he had been punished for his conceit. He was so ashamed that he stayed in the lonely desert for the rest of his life, without friends among either gods or mortals.

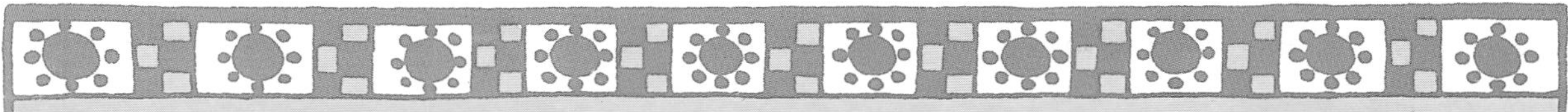

THE FOUR WINDS

Once the North, South, East, and West winds had belonged to Hera. But Zeus did not want his wife to have a power that he did not share, so he stole the winds away and tied them up in a leather bag until he could decide what to do with them.

Among the mortals on earth, there was a man named Aeolus, who had always worshiped Zeus faithfully. Zeus decided to reward him. One day he appeared to Aeolus and said, "Since you have always worshiped me loyally, I am going to let you live forever, like a god. And I am going to give you a job to do forever, just like a god's."

And then Zeus added, "But don't forget—you must go on making offerings to me and worshiping me as a mortal worships a god!"

And Aeolus promised that he would.

Then Zeus gave him the bag containing the four winds. He also gave Aeolus an island with steep cliffs and a dark cave in the cliffs where he was to keep the winds locked up until they were needed.

The island that Zeus gave to Aeolus was like no other island in the world. It did not stay in one spot but floated from place to place in the sea, and no one ever visited it.

Aeolus did his duty as Zeus had ordered. He tended to the winds and kept them locked in the cave until they were needed somewhere by mortals or the gods.

Each wind had a name. Boreas was the North Wind. He was the most famous of the winds because he was the most dangerous. Sailors always made offerings of sweet wine and roasted meat to Boreas before they set off on a long voyage. That was to bribe him to treat them kindly. Zephyrus was the West Wind. He was usually a friendly and playful wind, although he was somewhat unpredictable. The hot South Wind was called Notus, and the sweet-smelling East Wind was called Eurus.

Aeolus was always able to make Zephyrus, Notus, and Eurus do as he told them. But Boreas was like a naughty child and often insisted on having his own way. Even Aeolus could not always control this wildest of the winds.

THE CRUEL MOTHER

Hera, the wife of Zeus, was a very great and beautiful goddess. But she was also vain, cruel, and jealous. When her baby son, Hephaestus, was born, he was so puny and homely that none of the other gods and goddesses could manage to say "How beautiful your baby is!" and sound as though they were telling the truth.

One day when Hera was looking at the little baby lying in her arms, she said, "How could such a beautiful goddess as I am have such an ugly baby? You are certainly the ugliest baby I have ever seen!"

And right then, for no one was watching, Hera let little Hephaestus fall out of her lap. He fell from Mount Olympus and tumbled down, down through the clouds. Fortunately for him, he did not land on the hard and stony earth but fell into the blue sea and was not hurt.

Some kind water nymphs found the poor little baby god. They brought him home to their coral cave at the bottom of the sea and took good care of him. When Hephaestus was only a little boy, they gave him a workbench and forge and taught him to use them. He quickly grew beyond his teachers in skill. Soon he was creating wonderful things out of metal—things that had never been made before.

He fashioned a beautiful piece of jewelry of gold and silver, coral and pearls for Thetis, one of his foster mothers. From high on her throne on Mount Olympus, his real mother, the goddess Hera, saw the jewel shining in the sea. She immediately became jealous and wished she could have jewelry that extraordinary. So Hephaestus, even though he was still a very homely little boy, was summoned back to Mount Olympus.

Zeus gave him the job of making tools and armor and jewels and playthings for all the gods and goddesses. This job was so important that Hephaestus was given a golden throne, like the other Olympians.

Hera never did treat her son with any love or kindness. Nevertheless, Hephaestus always took his mother's side in her frequent quarrels with her husband. During one such quarrel, Zeus grew unusually furious at Hephaestus for defending his mother. Mighty Zeus picked up the young man and hurled him through the clouds like a thunderbolt.

This time Hephaestus was not as lucky as before, for he did not land in the soft waves of the sea. Instead he fell to earth, and both his legs were broken in the fall. But he was so skilled at metal work that he made a pair of golden braces for his legs. With these he could walk, although with a bad limp. Slowly Hephaestus made his way back up to his workshop and forge on Mount Olympus. From that time on, he kept busy at his craft and out of the quarrels between his parents.

At this time, there were only eleven Olympians. But one day, from out of a bright and foamy sea wave, a beautiful new goddess was born. Since she was naked, the gentle winds brought clothes for her to wear. Her name was Aphrodite, and she became the goddess of love and beauty.

With the gentle winds to guide her, Aphrodite came to Mount Olympus. Doves and sparrows flew beside her, and flowers sprouted wherever she stepped. As soon as Zeus saw her, he knew she would bring trouble. She was so beautiful that he was afraid all the gods would fall in love with her and quarrels would break out among them. He decided it would be best if she were married, and he chose homely Hephaestus for her husband.

It was not a bad marriage, as arranged marriages go, but Aphrodite did not love her husband. Instead, she adored cruel and handsome Ares, the god of war. Ares returned her passion, although he did not care for Aphrodite nearly as much as he enjoyed making war.

The fact that his wife loved another god did not keep Hephaestus from his work. Because it was difficult for him to move around, he invented golden tripods that held whatever tools he needed and came to him when he called. He also invented golden robots that looked like women. These mechanical golden women also came when he called and helped him in his work. Their hands were as skilled as those of any artist.

Whenever and wherever mortals made or used tools, they always asked Hephaestus to guide their minds and hands.

Hephaestus was also generous in sharing the secrets of how he made such marvels with Athene, his best friend among the Olympians. Unlike Hephaestus, who preferred to stay in his workshop on Mount Olympus, Athene liked to drop in on mortals she especially cared for. Athene enjoyed the people who lived in towns and cities and met together in the marketplaces. She taught some of the clever ones the secrets of Hephaestus's inventions. Some of these mortals became almost as inventive and skilled as Hephaestus himself.

THE BOY WHO FLEW

One of Athene's pupils was a man called Daedalus. Even though he was mortal, he was almost as remarkable an inventor and craftsman as the god Hephaestus. He became famous throughout the world.

In the island kingdom of Crete, there was a monster that belonged to King Minos and Queen Pasiphae. This monster had the head of a bull and the body of a man. It was cruel and dangerous, and it was called the Minotaur. Worse yet, it was the child of the queen. King Minos asked Daedalus to come to his kingdom and build something that would imprison the Minotaur within the palace walls.

Daedalus came to Crete, bringing his young son, Icarus, with him. Inside the palace walls, he built a marvelous maze. This maze had such complicated passageways that the monster could not find its way out.

But Daedalus soon discovered that, each year, the Minotaur needed to kill twelve youths and maidens from the city of Athens. Each year, twelve fine young men and women from Athens were sent to Crete to die in the maze. Daedalus did not want his work to be used for murder, so he helped one of the young men who came to die to save himself and his companions and to kill the Minotaur.

Queen Pasiphae was very angry because, as its mother, she loved the Minotaur, terrible as it had been. Her husband, in order to soothe her, decided to punish Daedalus. He made Daedalus and his son prisoners.

No captain of any ship that sailed to Crete dared take them away because the king had decreed that the inventor and his son could never leave the island. They lived in an isolated tower, where Daedalus had a simple workshop. They had only the sea-gulls for company. How Daedalus yearned to show Icarus the world beyond their island prison!

One day as Daedalus was watching the gulls wheeling and circling above the surf, he had an inspiration. He shouted down to his son, who was gathering shells on the lonely beach, "Minos may rule the sea, but he does not rule the air!"

Daedalus had observed how the gulls' wings were shaped, and how they worked. No mortal had ever before figured out how a bird could fly, but Daedalus thought he understood.

He and Icarus began to collect all the gull feathers they could find along the beach. They gathered the large, stiff ones and the tiny, light, downy ones that floated in the breeze. They saved the wax that honeybees made. Then Daedalus made wings of the seagull feathers and the beeswax for himself and Icarus. He worked long and patiently, and Icarus helped him, always doing what his father told him to do.

After they had made two pairs of long, curved wings, Daedalus made two harnesses of leather. He showed Icarus how to place the wings on his shoulders. Then he showed him how to run along the beach until he caught the wind and, like a seagull, flew up into the air.

Father and son practiced together until, one day, Daedalus decided it was time for them to leave the island. As they rose into the air and headed away from their island prison toward the sea, Daedalus called out to Icarus, "Follow me! Do not fly too low, or you will lose the air and sink into the waves. But do not fly too high, or the heat from the sun will melt the beeswax."

"Yes, Father," shouted Icarus above the sea noises and the wailing of the seagulls who flew beside him.

Higher and higher they flew. At last, Daedalus said, "We will stay at this level all the way. Remember what I told you — follow me!"

As they flew by, fishermen dropped their nets in wonder and farmers stopped at their plows. They thought they were seeing two gods in flight, for surely only gods could fly.

Icarus began to feel more and more sure of himself. He flew upward, then downward. He swooped and soared like a gull, laughing joyously as he did so. He cried out, "Look at me, Father!" and soared upward.

Daedalus beckoned him down, but Icarus thought, He is old and timid while I am young and strong. Surely I can fly a little better than he. Suddenly the boy disappeared into a cloud and flew up and up and up, higher and higher.

Too late, he saw feathers begin to fall from his wings. As the hot sun melted the wax, more and more feathers dropped away. Frantically, the boy flapped his arms in the air, but he could not fly without the wings. Instead, he dropped down and down until he fell into the sea and drowned.

Daedalus flew up in search of his son, calling as he went, "Icarus! Come down to me!"

Then he saw the telltale feathers drifting past him, and he heard the distant splash as Icarus fell into the sea. The old man cried as he continued on his journey, but he flew to freedom. He never made wings for anyone again.

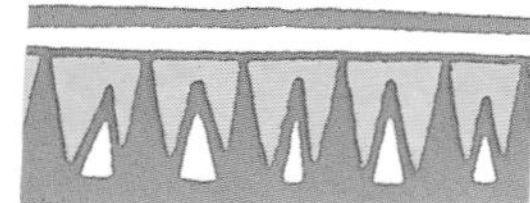

THE GIRL WHO WON ALL THE RACES

The gods and goddesses often liked to sit together around the glowing hearth that Hestia tended for them and tell stories. Just as mortals enjoyed stories of the gods, so did the gods like stories about the mortals they had befriended. This is a favorite story of Aphrodite's because of the part she played in it.

Atalanta was born a princess. But her father, the king, was so disappointed because she was not a boy that he ordered she be taken from her mother's arms and left alone in the hills to die.

The little baby princess did not die, however. Instead, a good and kind she-bear with cubs of her own found her. The mother bear treated Atalanta exactly as she did her own cubs, and Atalanta grew up to be as strong and fearless as her adopted brothers and sisters.

Artemis, the great goddess of the hunt, looked out for the child, too, for she was the protector of lost children. When Atalanta grew older, Artemis saw to it that she was befriended by a band of hunters. The hunters taught the young girl to use a bow and arrow and to run as fast as the wind.

Atalanta became braver and stronger and swifter than any young man in the world and performed many heroic deeds. At last, she returned to her father's palace and told him that she was the daughter he had left to die.

Her father realized that this courageous and strong young woman was certainly worthy of being his heir — as worthy as any son might have been. Besides, he still did not have a son. He welcomed Atalanta back to the palace on one condition.

"It is not suitable that you should be fighting battles and competing at sports and the hunt with men. You will be a queen one day, and you must have a husband to rule with you," said the king.

Atalanta had no wish to marry. She loved her free life in the forest. She did not want to sit indoors among the palace women, as her mother did, spinning and dyeing wool and weaving tapestries and telling stories day and night.

So Atalanta said to her father, "Very well, I will marry, as you wish. But I will only marry a man who can run faster than I can. For surely, Father, you would not want a son-in-law who is weaker than his wife?"

The king thought about this and agreed. He added an even sterner condition of his own, for he was by nature a cruel and demanding man. He decreed that any young man who ran a race against his daughter and lost would be put to death. In this way, he hoped to discourage all weak and cowardly suitors.

Sad to say, the girl won every race, and many fine and brave young men were put to death.

This made the goddess Aphrodite very unhappy, for she loved to see mortals in love with each other and happy together. She decided to take the situation in hand.

One day a prince came from a faraway land to race with Atalanta. It promised to be a close race, for this young man was a famous runner. As usual, judges were chosen to decide the winner. One of the judges was a young man named Hippomenes. Hippomenes was no runner himself, and on his way to the judging he thought how foolish it was for young men to risk their lives for any princess. But he could not know what the goddess Aphrodite had in mind.

Under Aphrodite's influence, Hippomenes took one look at Atalanta and fell in love. He thought at once that this brave girl would make a wonderful wife. To Hippomenes, her beauty was even more evident in the running clothes she wore, which revealed so much of her strong, muscular, and beautiful body.

Forgetting himself completely, Hippomenes suddenly said, "I will race the princess!"

His parents began to weep. Atalanta glanced at the young man who so foolishly wanted to race with her and thought to herself, What a pity that such a kind-looking and handsome young man must die. (This, too, was Aphrodite's doing.)

No one in the crowd that had gathered to watch the race knew why the princess who could not be beaten wiped a tear from her eye.

As soon as Hippomenes had said good-bye to his friends and family, Aphrodite appeared to him and said, "Hippomenes, I have three gifts for you. They will make you the winner in this race, I promise."

Then Aphrodite gave Hippomenes three golden apples that she had grown in her own orchard.

"Do as I tell you," said Aphrodite. "As the race goes on, you will fall behind Atalanta, no matter how hard you try to keep

up with her. Each time she passes you, throw one golden apple ahead of her. Believe me, she will not be able to resist it. You will see—you will win."

Then the goddess smiled sweetly at Hippomenes and vanished as quickly as she had come.

Right from the start, Atalanta ran ahead of Hippomenes. But he did as the goddess told him and threw out the first golden apple. Atalanta barely hesitated, but she knelt to pick it up. While she knelt, Hippomenes gained a few seconds and caught up closer behind her.

As the race continued, he threw out the second golden apple. This time he threw it a little to the side. Atalanta had to stop running for a moment to pick it up, but pick it up she did. As she stopped to pick up the second golden apple, Hippomenes ran right up beside her, and they raced along next to each other. All the judges held their breath in amazement as the young man ran a closer race with the princess than any suitor had ever run.

As they neared the finish line, Atalanta gained again on Hippomenes. But the goddess had instructed him well. Almost at the end of the race, Hippomenes threw the last golden apple.

That last apple landed well to the side of the racecourse. Atalanta gasped when she saw the beautiful golden toy shining in the grass. Then she looked ahead of her toward the finish line, which lay so close.

But Atalanta could not resist the golden apple, for this was Aphrodite's doing, so she went out of her way and stooped to pick it up. While she stopped, she took a second to catch her breath. And as she did, Hippomenes reached the finish line and the crowd cheered him loudly.

So Atalanta had to marry Hippomenes, but she was not

sorry at all. When their baby, a little boy called Parthenopaeus, was born, Atalanta heard the old nurse-women cooing and singing to him, and she said to her husband, "That is no way to bring up a child! I will not have our son grow into a spoiled and silly little prince. I want him brought up as I was!"

So Atalanta and Hippomenes took their little son to the very place where Atalanta's father had left her to die when she was a baby. Atalanta whistled and made some odd grunts and growls and waited.

Before long, Atalanta's bear foster-mother shuffled out of the forest.

"Don't be afraid," Atalanta whispered to her husband.

Then she handed their little baby boy to the big, furry she-bear. The bear took the baby in her arms and disappeared into the forest.

And this was the will of the goddess Artemis, as well.

Parthenopaeus grew up to be as brave and strong and swift as his mother. He became a great and famous hero. His parents were very proud of him, and his grandparents were, too, though Aphrodite and Artemis sometimes argued over who should take the credit for his glory.

PANDORA'S BOX

Pandora was made, not born as other people are. Hephaestus modeled her out of clay. He made her a young woman as beautiful as his wife, Aphrodite, the goddess of love and beauty.

Each of the gods and goddesses gave Pandora a gift. Then Athene, the goddess of wisdom, breathed life into her. Most of the gifts the gods gave her were good ones. But unfortunately Hermes, as always full of tricks and mischief, gave her more curiosity than was good for her.

Pandora was sent to live on earth. She had no trouble finding a good husband, for the gods and goddesses had given her the gifts of smiles and sweetness and wit and winning ways. Besides that, she was rich, for as a wedding gift the gods and goddesses gave her a box that had been made by Hephaestus. It was as beautiful as Pandora and very valuable, too.

"Never, never open that box!" all the gods and goddesses warned Pandora. She promised to obey them, but as time went on Pandora grew more and more curious about what was in the box that she had promised never to open.

In those days, there was no sadness among the mortals on

earth. And why should it have been otherwise? There was no sickness, no hunger, no jealousy, no laziness, no greed, no anger, no cruelty. Even death was like a long and gentle sleep when people were very tired. There was no suffering of any kind.

Perhaps things would have remained that way if tricky Hermes had not given Pandora so much curiosity. But every day Pandora grew more and more curious about just what was in

that box. At last, when she could no longer sleep for wondering what her box contained, she said to herself early one morning, "I will just take a little peek!"

So she opened the box, just to take a little peek. And out of that box flew dreadful things. Greed and Envy came out first and soared up into the clean, bright air. Pandora tried to slam the box shut, but she could not. Out flew Hatred and Cruelty with terrible force. Hunger and Poverty followed. Then Sickness came, and Despair, and all the other terrible things that the gods and goddesses knew should remain safely hidden in that box.

Pandora had set them all free.

"Come back! Come back where you belong!" Pandora called out to the terrible things as they flew around her. She grabbed at them in the air, but they soared out of her reach and up into the sky. None came back. They are still out there bringing misery and trouble to people on earth.

But the gods and goddesses had not put only dreadful things in Pandora's box. Hidden in among the terrible things was something small and fragile-winged and good. This thing was Hope. Who was the kindly god or goddess who thought to put Hope in among all the miseries and misfortunes? No one knows.

But because Hope was hidden in Pandora's box, whenever there is too much trouble and sadness among us mortals, Hope makes us think that tomorrow will be better.

And soon Pandora dried her tears.

"I hope I will never be too curious again!" she said.

And she never was.

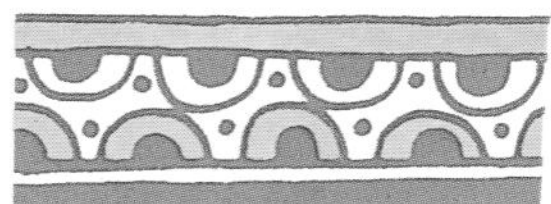

THE BRIDE WHO STEPPED ON A SNAKE

Orpheus played the lyre so beautifully that everyone was sure he had been taught to play by Apollo, the god of music. They were right: Not only had Apollo taught his art to Orpheus, but he had also given him a lyre to play. It was only natural that Orpheus could compose the loveliest songs ever created by a mortal. After all, his mother was Calliope, the greatest of the Muses. She was also the Muse of epic poetry.

Whatever the reasons, there never had been a musician like Orpheus. His songs were so beautiful and the sounds he plucked from his lyre so enchanting that not only people but wild beasts of the forests and even trees and rocks danced to his music.

Orpheus fell in love with a very young and beautiful nymph named Eurydice. Eurydice loved him as well, and they decided to marry.

On their wedding day, all was perfect except for one thing. The torches that should have burned steadily and brightly throughout the ceremony sizzled and smoked instead. The wedding guests rubbed their stinging eyes and whispered in alarm that this was a sign sent from the gods. It meant that all would not go well in the marriage of Orpheus and Eurydice.

As soon as Orpheus and Eurydice had been married, something horrible did happen. Eurydice was bitten on the foot by a poisonous snake and quickly died.

Brokenhearted Orpheus wandered throughout the world until he found the entrance to Hades's underworld kingdom of the dead. Orpheus did not want life without his beloved Eurydice, and so he entered the dreaded kingdom of Hades.

A strange and frightful dog named Cerberus guarded the entrance. Cerberus looked like no dog ever seen. He had three heads, each uglier and crueler than the others, and a tail made of poisonous, hissing snakes. Each of the beast's three heads barked, snarled, growled, and bared its teeth at Orpheus. But Orpheus knew songs and melodies that could charm wild beasts, and so he played his lyre and sang to Cerberus.

The terrifying dog stopped growling and baring its teeth. It lowered each of its three heads and wagged its tail. Cerberus grunted gently with pleasure.

Charon, the ferryman who carried the dead across the River Styx on their way to the underworld, was also enchanted by Orpheus's song. He took pity on the grieving musician and carried him across that dreadful river, even though Orpheus was still full of youth and health and life.

Searching for Eurydice, Orpheus traveled past the bloodless ghosts of all the mortals who had ever died. Even these ghosts

began to cry as they listened to Orpheus sing of his longing for dead Eurydice. On and on he journeyed, until at last he reached the thrones of the dreaded god Hades and his sad queen, Persephone.

When he came face-to-face with the great god of the underworld, Orpheus composed a song especially for him. He sang of how he knew that mortals were not meant to live forever, as the gods did. But he sang of how short Eurydice's time on earth had been and how much joy had been taken from him by her death. He reminded Hades of the loneliness he himself felt when his queen was not with him. The song Orpheus sang was so moving that Hades began to weep. He forgot for the moment that he was the god who never showed pity either for the dead or for the loved ones they left behind.

Soon, from among the shadowy ghosts in the damp and murky darkness, Orpheus saw someone coming toward him. She moved slowly, for she was limping, but her hand was held out to him. It was Eurydice.

Hades told Orpheus he would grant his request. He would let Eurydice return to the land of the living and live out her life as Orpheus's wife. But even though Hades had cried the first tears of pity he had ever known, he was still the harsh and stern god of the dead.

"I will let your wife follow you back to the sunshine of earth," he said. "You may stay together until old age brings each of you back to me, on one condition. You must promise, Orpheus, not to look at Eurydice until you leave my kingdom. If you do, she will return to me forever, and I will not allow you to remain here with her, for your time has not come."

Orpheus was overjoyed to hear what Hades said, and he

promised to do as the god commanded. Quickly he turned from the pitiful sight of pale and bloodless Eurydice. He sang as he led her through the damp darkness, and Eurydice followed his voice and the music of his lyre.

The journey was long and terrifying for Orpheus. Other ghosts pulled at him and tried to draw him back among them, but Orpheus kept his promise. He did not look back but trusted his music to bring Eurydice with him.

At last Orpheus reached the River Styx. Charon, who was always obedient to Hades, offered to ferry them across. And as he boarded the boat, Orpheus still did not look to make sure Eurydice was following him. He kept on singing and plucking at his lyre. Even when Orpheus saw the three-headed dog on the other side of the river, he did not look behind him.

When they reached the other side, Orpheus stepped off the ferryboat. Suddenly he saw a little slash of sunlight. He thought he was out of the kingdom of Hades, at last, and turned his head to make sure that Eurydice was behind him.

Poor Orpheus. She was behind him, but he had been mistaken. They were not yet out of the land of the dead.

Orpheus heard Eurydice whisper, "Good-bye, my love. . . ."

He dropped his lyre. He reached out wildly toward the darkness to hold her in his arms one last time, but his arms held nothing. Eurydice had vanished like the ghost she was.

Orpheus begged Charon to take him back across the River Styx, but the ferryman, ever loyal to his lord, would not. There were no songs that Orpheus could sing to make the ferryman obey him.

So Orpheus sang no more. Instead, he sat upon the riverbank, sobbing and cursing the god of the dead. He did not eat, he did not sleep, and he did not wash his face. But curse as he might, Hades did not respond. And the louder the shouts of Orpheus became, the greater was the silence in the world of the dead. Eurydice did not return.

Finally Orpheus gave up. With unbearable sadness, he left the kingdom of Hades, but he took his lyre with him.

Was it the will of Apollo that made Orpheus play again? For, in time, he sang and played his lyre, and he sang and played more beautifully than ever before. His grief and suffering had made his art even greater.

There was such beauty in his new music that green hills and mountains solemnly moved from where they were and danced in lovely patterns. Trees, birds, and beasts joined the hills and mountains in the dance, and Apollo looked down on his pupil with even greater joy and pleasure.

But Orpheus never stopped mourning the loss of Eurydice, and he never loved another woman.

THE NYMPH WHO HAD THE LAST WORD

Hera was always trying to catch Zeus with another woman. Even though it was Hera's nature to be demanding and jealous, the truth is that Zeus was frequently guilty of the things that she suspected. One day she heard through some Olympian gossip that Zeus was planning to go dancing in a wooded grove with a group of pretty nymphs.

"I will catch him this time!" she said angrily, and raced down to the forest where she was sure she would find her husband.

The nymphs had heard that Hera was coming, and they were afraid of what she would do to them for entertaining Zeus. So they sent one of their band to meet Hera on her way to the lovely grove where Zeus and the others were having a party. The nymph's name was Echo, and she was not only pretty, as all nymphs were, but a chatterbox as well.

Echo saw Hera marching purposefully toward her in all her grandeur. Echo pretended not to know who the goddess was and began to talk to her, prattling on about this, that, and the other thing. As the silly nymph talked on endlessly, Hera grew very annoyed, for the girl's chatter was delaying her. Finally she said, "Oh, be quiet, you silly girl!"

But there had been a purpose to Echo's tireless conversation. While she had been talking to Hera and dancing and skipping in front of her on the path, the other nymphs had run away and Zeus had returned to Mount Olympus. By the time Hera reached the place where she had expected to find her husband, everyone was gone. Hera suspected rightly that Echo had played a trick on her.

"Ah!" said the goddess sarcastically to the pretty nymph. "You seem to enjoy having the last word! Well, the last word is what you shall always have!"

And to this day, poor little Echo must always repeat the last word she hears. Next time you are in a place beloved by the nymphs and Zeus, just try calling, "Echo, can you hear me?"

And Echo will answer you by saying, "Me? . . . me? . . . me? . . ." and that is all.

THE HUNTER AND HIS HOUNDS

Artemis was the twin sister of Apollo. Just as the sun and light were Apollo's, the moon and the dark, shadowy forests belonged to Artemis. This is how it came to be.

When Artemis was very little, she was great Zeus's favorite child. One day the small goddess said to her father, "Father, when I grow up I do not ever want to get married. Instead, I wish to have a silver bow and arrows and a short yellow tunic with scarlet trim and sturdy boots like hunters wear. Because, dear Father, I want to be the goddess of the hunt! I want to be in charge of all the wild beasts of the forest and to live among them always. I want to be in charge of the waxing and waning of the moon, too. And if you make me goddess of the forest and the hunt and the moon, I will need some helpers. I would like a band of little girls to help me. In return, I promise that although I will never be a mother myself, I will help women when they are having babies and look after children as well. Please, Father!"

Because Zeus adored his little daughter, he gave her everything she asked for.

Few mortals ever saw Artemis, for she was the shyest of the gods and goddesses. She stayed hidden in the deepest forests with

her band of little girls and the wild beasts. But whenever Zeus called a council of the twelve Olympians, she always came to her throne, carrying her silver bow like a crescent moon and wearing her bright yellow and scarlet hunting tunic. She was as beautiful as her twin brother was handsome.

Whenever hunters entered the dark forests that were the domain of Artemis, they always made an offering to her, so that she would look kindly upon them and allow them to go home carrying meat for their people. However, terrible things could happen to any mortal who angered Artemis, even unintentionally. This is such a story.

Actaeon was a hunter. He loved to go into the forest with his friends and a group of strong, brave, and obedient hounds that helped him run down the swift deer. He always made offerings to Artemis, and he was always successful in the hunt.

One day Actaeon paused in the forest to rest. As he sat on a log under the huge green trees that hid the sky, he suddenly heard water tinkling and splashing and the laughing voices of many little girls. He tiptoed through the forest to see where the laughter was coming from.

Actaeon peered around the wide trunk of a great oak tree. He saw a spring that spouted up and made a pool. Then he saw something no hunter was meant to see.

The goddess Artemis was taking her bath in the pool. She had taken off her yellow and scarlet hunting tunic and her sturdy boots. She had put her clothes with her silver bow and arrows on the mossy banks of the pool. The little girls who always attended her surrounded her in the pool, laughing and splashing as children do. They bathed the goddess, their leader, with sweet-smelling mosses and pine needles.

As quietly as he could, Actaeon moved a little closer to the pool. But the poor hunter stepped on a branch, which cracked and made a loud and sudden noise that could be heard over the laughter and the chatter and the splashing, tinkling water.

The goddess gave a quick cry of alarm and turned to see where the sound came from. Before the hunter could run and hide, she saw him. Her helpers surrounded her in the pool and tried to hide her, but she was so much taller than the tallest of them that they could not conceal her nakedness.

The goddess was very, very angry. She reached for her silver bow and arrows to shoot the hunter through the heart, but they lay beyond her reach on the mossy bank. So she splashed water from the pool on Actaeon, screaming as she did so, "Now

try to tell your friends that you have seen the goddess Artemis naked in her bath, if you can ever speak again!"

No sooner had the water splashed upon Actaeon than horns sprouted from his head. The horns grew quickly and branched into great antlers. His nose and mouth grew velvety and soft. His body soon was covered in deer-colored fur. When he ran in terror from the angry goddess, he ran on the four legs of a stag.

Actaeon's hounds saw a stag running and did not recognize their master. They did exactly what hunting dogs are trained to do. They chased the stag and ran it down, encircled it, and leaped upon it to kill it. Actaeon cried out by name to each hound that he had raised from a puppy. But the sounds that came from his velvety muzzle were only the pitiful cries of a dying beast.

None of his friends ever knew what had become of Actaeon, for they could not find him in the dark forest, and he did not answer when they called him. They had no idea that the fine stag that Actaeon's hounds had killed and they carried home from the forest had been their friend and companion.

THE GOD WHO WAS KIDNAPPED BY PIRATES

Dionysus was the son of Zeus and a mortal woman. When he was a young boy, he traveled as far away as India and Egypt, and farther still. Wherever he went, he taught people how to plant and cultivate grapevines. Then he taught them to harvest the purple grapes that grew in the vineyards and to make sweet wine from the grapes.

Dionysus was an extraordinarily handsome boy. He wore his hair in long black curls. He had eyes the color of the sea. He wore a grape-colored cape over his shoulders and carried a walking staff to help him over rough and stony places on his journeys. The staff had a pinecone at the top, and shiny ivy twirled around it.

Sometimes the young god traveled with a large troop of companions. Some of these companions were Maenads, mortal women who dressed in the skins of wild beasts. Maenads danced as though they were insane and beat fiercely on their tambourines. People were afraid of them, and they had reason to be.

Since Dionysus was still a boy, he also traveled with his tutor, old Silenus, who had a face wrinkled from years of laughter. Silenus had the ears of a horse and a horse's tail and the fattest belly ever seen. Many Satyrs also traveled with Dionysus. They looked as Silenus had looked when he was young, but, unlike him, they were not fat and lazy. They were as wild and full of pranks as the Maenads were of madness. They played shrill, harsh melodies on flutes and danced and danced.

But there were many times when Dionysus left his friends behind and traveled alone. This story took place when the young god was alone.

One day Dionysus fell asleep at the edge of a wild and desolate seashore. He did not know that while he slept so soundly a pirate ship was on its way to that very shore. The pirates knew they could find a freshwater spring in that faraway place.

A group of them, including the captain, came ashore. No sooner had they spotted the sleeping boy, so extraordinarily handsome and richly clothed in his purple cape, than they nodded to one another in their wicked, conspiratorial way. Each pirate knew what the other meant. Quickly and roughly they grabbed the sleeping Dionysus and hauled him off to their ship, which lay sloshing about in the waves just offshore.

"What a prize this boy is!" said the captain to his sailors. "Just look at his fine clothes and shining curls! He looks well fed. I am sure he is the son of some foreign king who will pay a good ransom for him. We just have to find out where he comes from and set sail for there. Then I will tell his rich parents we have him and demand a good price for his safe return."

And the pirate sailors thought to themselves, If we do not find his family, we can surely sell him for a good price in some slave market.

They took strong rope and began to tie the sleepy boy to the mast of their ship. At that moment, Dionysus woke fully and stared at them with his sea-colored eyes. And when he looked directly into the eyes of the helmsman who steered the ship, the helmsman cried out, "Let him go! Don't you see? This is no king's mortal son, but a god we have kidnapped. Perhaps he is Zeus himself or Poseidon who rules the sea and makes the tempests toss ships and blow them over when he is angry. I do not know which god he is, but god he must be. Let him go!"

But the captain shouted, "You stupid fool! Don't you see what a good wind is coming up? Raise the sails, grab the oars, and let's be on our way before someone comes looking for him! Quickly, sailors, finish tying him up!"

The pirates tried to obey their captain and continued to

wrap strong ropes around Dionysus and the mast. But as quickly as they wrapped, the ropes broke. And before the sailors' eyes, the ropes changed into vines of shining green ivy. The ivy vines twisted around the mast and across the decks and around the oars so the ship could not move. Where the mast had been, there hung an enormous grapevine with curling tendrils. Heavy purple grapes hung among the curls on the young prisoner's head. Bright berries and beautiful flowers sprouted and blossomed in the ivy. A wild, strange, and frightening music of flutes and tambourines could be heard, although from where the music came, no one knew. Purple, sweet-smelling wine flowed over the ship's decks, but from where it came, no one knew. The pirates were terrified.

As if these things were not miracle enough, suddenly the boy prisoner vanished into the wind. In his place stood an enormous lion, roaring loudly. Amidships there appeared a huge, shaggy bear standing erect on its hind legs. The bear growled and the lion roared in time to the eerie music of the flutes and the tambourines.

As wine flowed into the sea, the ship stood locked in ivy, grapevines, and dreadful noises. The pirate crew ran whimpering toward the helmsman who had, after all, warned them.

Only the captain remained where he was. Suddenly the lion leaped upon him and grabbed him with sharp claws, just as the captain and his sailors had grabbed the sleeping boy. The captain shrieked with pain and horror before he died.

When the pirates heard the captain's cry, they quickly jumped overboard into the sparkling sea, where they immediately turned into dolphins. The young god had taken pity on them, cruel though they had been to him.

Only the helmsman stayed on the ship. The lion turned back into Dionysus. The grapevines disappeared as suddenly as they had come, and wind filled the sail. Ivy vines no longer twisted among the oars. Wine no longer flowed along the decks. The huge, shaggy bear was gone, and the wild music of flutes and tambourines could no longer be heard. All was silent except for the gentle lapping of the waves against the ship and the soft whistling and swishing of the dolphins who swam alongside.

Then Dionysus spoke to the helmsman, who knelt on deck, awestruck and trembling. His face was hidden in the palms of his hands. He was too frightened to look at this powerful god who could work such miracles.

"Don't be afraid," said Dionysus. "You have pleased me. I am Dionysus, the son of Zeus himself. Because you alone of all your companions knew me to be a god, your life will be long and joyous. You will never need to fear, for I will always be your friend."

Then the handsome boy smiled as sweetly as the child he was, and the helmsman was no longer afraid.

Wherever he went, the helmsman told the story of how the god Dionysus had been kidnapped by pirates. Everyone who listened and believed his story was favored by Dionysus, the most mysterious of all the gods.

THE KING WHO WISHED FOR GOLD

When Prince Midas was a baby sleeping in his cradle, a parade of little ants climbed across his plump cheeks and placed grains of shining yellow wheat upon his smiling lips. His royal parents sent for a soothsayer, who told them that this omen meant that the little prince would someday be a very rich man. But the soothsayer did not tell how or when this would happen.

When Midas was grown and had become king, he planted a wonderful rose garden that became very famous. All kinds of fragrant and colorful roses grew in his garden. There was nothing the king loved so much as to prune his roses. But he sometimes thought of the great riches that had been foretold for him and wondered where they were.

One morning a group of his gardeners came to the king. They brought with them a fat old man who had chains of roses from the king's garden draped around him. He had been found sleeping among the king's rosebushes, and it was easy to tell from the way he staggered and the way he smelled that he had drunk far too much wine the night before.

King Midas did not punish the old man for trespassing, however. He recognized the drunken old fellow by his fat belly and his horse's ears and tail. This was none other than Silenus, the tutor of the young god of wine, Dionysus. King Midas wanted to stay on the good side of this powerful god, so he was extremely kind and hospitable to Silenus.

Silenus, for his part, kept King Midas enchanted by the stories he told. The stories that Midas loved best were the ones about a marvelous land that lay at the end of the ocean, behind Boreas, the North Wind. This land was inhabited by a very fortunate group of people who, when they reached old age, began to grow backward until they were babies again. Then they simply disappeared like seeds in the wind. Never in their long lives did they suffer any unhappiness at all. They were called the Hyperboreans, or the people who lived behind the North Wind.

King Midas enjoyed his fat and funny guest. But after ten days and ten nights of storytelling, he and a royal escort accompanied old Silenus to the place where his young pupil, Dionysus, was. Dionysus was so appreciative of the kindness the king had shown to his dear old tutor that he promised he would give Midas anything he wished.

Now although Midas was a comfortable king in a pleasant and prosperous land, the very great riches that had been foretold for him had never come his way, and he was no longer a young man. So the king wasted no time in saying to the god, "I wish that everything I touch would turn to gold!"

Dionysus was sorry that King Midas had made such a foolish wish, but he granted it, all the same.

On the way home, to test whether or not his wish had been granted, Midas broke a little green twig from an oak tree. The green wood changed immediately into precious gold. He picked up an ordinary stone. It turned into a heavy nugget of brightest gold. He picked an apple, and it, too, turned to gold. His heart was ready to burst with joy! Everything he touched turned to gold, just as Dionysus had promised it would.

As soon as he reached his palace, the king ordered a grand and extravagant feast to be set before him. All kinds of rare and expensive delicacies were prepared because Midas thought, After all, if I am so rich, why should I spare any expense?

And then he sat down to eat.

But the piece of bread he picked up hardened in his hand and turned to gold. Slices of meat became slabs of glimmering gold. He picked up his cup of wine, and slippery liquid gold gagged him so that he could not drink.

Poor King Midas realized that for all his newfound wealth he would soon starve to death if he could not eat or drink. Suddenly he hated the gift that he had wanted so much. He lifted his hands toward the sky and said, "Please, Lord Dionysus, forgive me for making such a foolish wish. I beg you, set me free from my own greed and stupidity!"

Dionysus was full of pity for the situation Midas had created for himself. Because he was a kindly and forgiving god, he immediately canceled the charm that had made everything King Midas touched turn to gold.

But he said to him, "Just to be sure that no trace of this charm remains, I want you to go and wash yourself at the source of the River Sardis. Where the spring spouts forth in clouds of spray, scrub your entire body and hair and beard until you wash all the gold away."

King Midas did as the god had told him. Dionysus had been right, for sprinkles of gold spangled the stream when he washed himself in it. To this day, gold flows through that river — the very gold that King Midas washed from himself.

From then on, King Midas was content with his rose garden and never again wished for gold and great wealth.

THE GOAT-FOOTED GOD

In his work as messenger from Zeus, the god Hermes spent more time among mortals on earth than he did among the other Immortal Ones on Mount Olympus. So it is not surprising that when he fell in love, it was with a mortal maiden, the beautiful daughter of King Dryops.

Tricky Hermes plotted a way to meet the princess without frightening her with his godliness. You must remember that even though Hermes was a young and handsome god, he was, nevertheless, the god who always accompanied dying mortals to the kingdom of Hades. For this reason, the sight of him was always frightening. So Hermes disguised himself as a shepherd and found work tending the sheep of King Dryops. That way he could see the princess every day when she came to the meadows with her ladies-in-waiting to play with the sweet little lambs in the flock.

Hermes knew how to flirt without seeming to do so. Before long, the beautiful princess fell in love with the handsome and intelligent shepherd.

The king saw that this shepherd was no ordinary man. He did not object when his daughter and the shepherd became lovers, for King Dryops was convinced that his shepherd was probably a king's son in disguise—perhaps hiding because of enemies in his father's court. And he did not even object when his daughter discovered she was going to have a baby.

The baby was born in the king's palace in the comfortable bed of the princess. The birth went quickly and well, but when the princess looked down at her baby son, she was horrified. For this baby looked nothing like his good-looking parents.

He had two little horns on his head like a goat. On his chin, there grew a short beard like a billy goat's. His arms, it is true, were cute and chubby, and he had dear little baby fingers on his hands. But his legs and feet were something else again! His legs were covered with coarse black hair like a goat's, and where his feet should have been there were cloven hooves. He had a little tail, too, that stuck up straight just like a goat's!

As soon as this baby looked up at his mother, he let out a loud "Ha! Haah!" that was a sound like nothing the princess had ever heard. She was so terrified that she jumped up from the bed and ran away screaming. Her nurses were quick to follow her.

But Hermes in his travels had seen many strange things. He looked at his little newborn son and said, like any proud father, "What a fine, strong, and funny little baby god you are!"

And the god Hermes tenderly wrapped the baby in a rabbit skin, all warm and cozy. Then he quickly clothed himself in his winged sandals and his winged cap and flew away from the kingdom of King Dryops. He flew straight up to Mount Olympus, carrying the baby in his arms.

The Immortal Ones were all happy to see Hermes again, for he had been away for an unusually long time. When they saw his strange little son, they all began to laugh. The goatish baby god laughed back even louder than Zeus himself, and the gods and goddesses were delighted. So, because he had pleased all of them, they decided to call him Pan, which means all.

Pan grew up with his father on Mount Olympus. He took after Hermes in his ability to tell jokes and funny stories. But unfortunately Pan's jokes were often rude and embarrassing ones. And he was noisy and boisterous and destructive — even Hermes could not deny that. Besides, he was always dirty, and he smelled like a goat. Despite all his faults, he was dearly loved by his father, and he was a close friend of Dionysus, the god of wine.

Hermes suggested to Zeus that Pan could help him in one of his many jobs. Since Hermes was god of all flocks, he asked Zeus if Pan could take over being god of the goats that grazed in the highest mountain pastures. Zeus agreed this was a good idea. He thought that such a job might keep wild and noisy Pan out of trouble.

To tell the truth, Pan much preferred his home in a cave in the mountain meadows to life on Mount Olympus where Zeus and the other gods and goddesses were always trying to make him behave himself.

Pan was a little lazy. The goats took care of themselves and jumped and frolicked in the meadows, while he slept during the hottest part of the day. This carefree life was exactly right for the goats and for Pan.

Occasionally some unlucky persons would climb up too high into the mountains. If they happened to disturb Pan at his long noonday nap, the suddenly awakened god would give a shout like the one that had frightened his lovely mother. When people, no matter how brave, heard that hair-raising sound—somewhat like a laugh and somewhat a sound like no other—they would become paralyzed with terror. Their hearts would begin to pound harder and harder. Their tongues would stick to the dry roofs of their mouths, and their knees would shake. When this happened, the victims knew that they had disturbed the goat-god, Pan. And they never returned to that place again.

As his father had before him, Pan fell in love one day. He loved a beautiful nymph called Syrinx, but she did not return his love. In fact, she was terrified of him. When Pan came running and shouting after her on his black, hairy goat legs, tripping and dancing on his cloven hooves, Syrinx ran from him. She ran and ran until she came to a sparkling mountain stream.

Many nymphs were the daughters of rivers and streams. When Syrinx came to this particular stream, she called out to her father in terror. Just before the lovesick god reached her, the nymph was changed into a bunch of tall reeds waving and rustling along the edge of the stream.

Pan howled in heartbreak, but he was determined that Syrinx would be his. So he cut down the graceful reeds that had been his one true love. Just as his father Hermes had made a lyre

from a tortoise shell, Pan made a set of flutelike pipes from the reeds. And he called the set of pipes he made a syrinx after the lovely nymph they had been.

Nothing was beautiful about Pan except the plaintive melodies he played upon his syrinx. But these melodies were as lovely as the songs of the birds in the high mountain glades. By moonlight, when they did not have to look at his ugly face and hairy body, lovely nymphs came and danced with Pan as the goat-footed god played on his pipes.

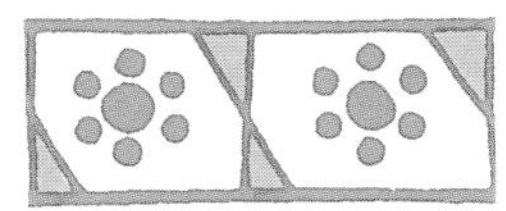

AUTHOR'S NOTE

I was lucky to hear these stories from my grandfather when I was a child. I was young enough to accept without question the wondrous tricks and transformations of the Greek gods and goddesses, and I acquired a love for stories about them that has lasted all my life. I wanted to create a book of Greek myths that would appeal to children as young as I was when I first heard them.

These myths have been told and retold by many authors through the centuries, and so a number of interpretations of each story have come down to us. In every case, I have chosen whatever I liked best from a variety of tellings as a basis for my own retelling.

I have depended principally upon the *Homeric Hymns*; Hesiod's *Theogony* and *Works and Days*; *The Library of Apollodorus*; and Ovid's *Metamorphoses*. Robert Graves's *The Greek Myths* has been a very helpful contemporary source, as has *The Oxford Companion to Classical Literature*. I had read these stories first in Bulfinch's *Mythology*, and so I returned to that as well.

Painters and sculptors throughout the history of Western art have been inspired by the Greek gods and goddesses. I have tried to portray them as I imagine them, but, of course, I have been helped by images as ancient as those painted on Greek vases and carved in Greek or Roman marble, and as recent as the beautiful drawings and prints of Pablo Picasso.